No More Limits

Breaking free from what stopped you to reach your potential.

Carlos Vargas

To Joshua, my first-born child.

The world changed forever the day

you were born.

I love you with all my heart

and I always will.

Contents

Acknowledgements

I have to say a huge thank you to all the wonderful people whose work has contributed to my own growth over the years and consequently ended up in this book in different forms.

Another huge thank you to my mentor, business partner, and friend: Carlos Peralta. His brilliant mind and encouragement are a constant source of inspiration to me.

Thank you to John Maxwell and the John Maxwell Team for pouring into lives so abundantly. His kindness, patience, and immense wisdom as a mentor and spiritual guide have changed me, my relationships, and the lives of my family beyond measure.

And last but not least God. You are the reason why I exist. Everything that I am, know, and have are blessings from You. Thank You for loving me so much.

About the author

For the last 20 years Carlos Vargas, has impacted people's lives through speaking, teaching, and inspiring individuals across Brazil, Mexico, Cuba, Puerto Rico, United States, and Europe. Carlos loves being a Transformation Agent for people who have current limiting beliefs in their business, personal, and spiritual lives. This is the fuel which keeps him going.

He works with individuals, families, groups, and businesses to help them reduce stress and enjoy life through great interaction via their personality and individual leadership competencies. His education began at the Defenders of the Faith Theological Institute in Santurce, Puerto Rico and later received over 80 IT certifications during his successful career as an International Architect with different Fortune 100 and 500 companies.

Carlos was part of an elite team of world changers invited to transform the lives of the country of Paraguay.

1

Introduction

Change always starts in your mind. The way you think determines the way you feel, and the way you feel influences the way you act.

                                        ~Rick Warren

The secret of change is to focus all your energy, not on fighting the old, but on building the new.

                                        ~ Socrates

A couple of months after my son Joshua's fifth birthday he was eating rice and beans for dinner. He loves to talk while eating and one of his questions this particular night was interesting. He asked where beans came from and how they grew. I showed him one of the beans from his plate and then showed him a dry bean from our pantry. He stopped what he was doing and then asked "Can I plant this bean so we can have a bean tree?"

If you have kids, you know they say the darndest things. Then he said: "...maybe when we plant the beans, they will grow into trees and our tree will grow all the way to the sky and... and... we can climb them..." I tried not to laugh because his idea was similar to a children's story book we had in the house, but he was being serious.

I didn't want to extinguish his enthusiasm, so I didn't tell him that this little bean was dead— or so I thought. He asked his mom if we could plant some beans so we could have bean trees. His mom agreed and they started to look for a gardening pot to plant the new bean trees.

A couple of minutes after he placed the beans in the potting soil he asked why they were not sprouting. I told him they needed time, water, and sunlight to grow. After I mentioned that the plants will needed water, Joshua took a twenty-ounce bottle of water and poured it all over them. "Maybe they're thirsty..." he told me.

The next day he came close to the gardening pot and looked at soil. "Why are they not coming out?" he asked.

"Patience my boy, patience," I told him. Immediately I thought of Mr. Miyagi from *The Karate Kid* saying, "wax on, wax of." He looked at me like I was crazy, but he would soon understand just what those words meant.

We sat down at the dining table and played chess. While playing, I tried explaining to him that everything worthwhile in life takes time.

Later in the day his mom decided to put the gardening pot outside, on the front porch, so that it would get sunlight while still being sheltered from the rain. Joshua was looking forward to seeing his new "bean trees" when they grew from the soil.

We were both delighted and amazed when the little bean sprouted in just a few days! His attention span, typical of most five-year-old boys, meant that within a minute of witnessing his bean's heroic struggle for life he was off playing his favorite video game while running around the house and chasing our dog.

While traveling that week, I sat and thought about that bean for some time though. While it was in the dry and closed kitchen pantry it was helpless. It would never grow into anything. It would never DO anything. It would just sit there.

But what really caught my attention was the fact that as soon as it was placed into an environment that was more conducive to its growth, it burst into life. It wasn't dead after all. The potential was obviously there all along, but you would have never known it if you had seen it packed in a bag on the shelf in the kitchen pantry.

Today that seedling has been moved into a little pot with some potting soil and is growing into multiple bean plants or, in Joshua's eyes, little bean trees—as he said in the beginning.

It is very natural for the seed to germinate and sprout. It's very natural for the seedling to grow into a little plant. And it's very natural for the plant to reach for the sky and grow as big as it possibly can. It doesn't take effort to grow. It does it because of what it is – a plant!

It may well have been more comfortable sitting on the kitchen pantry with nothing to do, but that's not what plants are supposed to do, is it? They're supposed to grow. And they're supposed to keep growing until they stop growing. And when they stop growing they die.

As I look back at my life, I realize that all too often I've been far too much like the seed stored in the kitchen pantry than the seedling in the pot! Not so much in later life, but certainly for vast stretches of my earlier life. If I was comfortable, I didn't want to move!

The trouble with this mindset is that no one else is going to move you. We all must paddle our own canoe. If you sit back and rest, then by default you'll begin to drift along with the flow instead of where you want to go. And water only ever flows downhill!

Everything worth having is uphill.
~John C. Maxwell

My friend and mentor, John Maxwell, says that everything worth having is uphill. And I think that most of us can recognize and accept that when we stop to think about it. When we're comfortable, we don't spend too much time thinking about what we want, where it is, or how we can get it. Instead, we focus on what we don't want and worrying about losing what we have.

Joshua's little bean plant has a very clear goal: to reach for the light. This goal is pursued relentlessly every single day of its life. Little wonder it makes such great progress.

If we all had such clear objectives and pursued them continually, I'm sure we would astound ourselves with what we are capable of.

Why don't more people make such great progress in their lives then? The statistics are staggeringly disappointing when you look at them. Only 5% of people ever reach financial independence. I read once that most people die within seven years of retiring. Almost everyone is unhappy in their job and nearly everyone argues about money!

Is this all we have to look forward to after a lifetime of experience? What happened to all those hopes and dreams we shared so freely as a child? Where did that hope and wonder of the world go? What happened to that daily happiness that seemed to ooze out of us, infecting everyone around us? Why is true happiness so evasive for so many and what do we have to do to get more of it?

Perhaps happiness is a childish fantasy, something that is not meant for grownups! As I sit here and glance over at Joshua's little sapling I can't help but wonder: Is it as happy as a toddler? Will it stop being happy when it reaches a certain size and then become a miserable, pessimistic, know-it-all adult; only to finally become a crooked, cranky old bean plant?

As I reviewed my notes while writing this chapter, a story from one of my favorite books came to mind. In John Maxwell's great book, *The 15 Invaluable Laws of Growth*, he tells a story that I love. A fortune teller reads a man's fortune and says, "You'll be poor and miserable until you are 40 years old." The man still has a glint of hope and asks what happens then. Her response: "Then you get used to it!"

I love the prophetic brilliance in that story – not for everyone of course, but for many people. It is sad but oh so true!

Thucydides said, "The secret to happiness is freedom. And the secrct to freedom is courage." Surely this applies to individuals just as much as it applies to nations, races or communities. How many people do you know who have the courage to pursue flexibility and freedom in their lives in an appropriate way? Do you think they are happy?

Another great source of guidance for people around the world says, "Straight is the gate and narrow is the way and few there be that find it." Could that mean peace and happiness is indeed a scarce thing?

A great mentor of mine said that happiness is an inside job. It's not something you get from external circumstances or things. It is the result of what's going on inside. He said that there is almost a 100% correlation between happiness and awareness of who you are. The more self-aware person can be happy almost completely detached from externals while the unaware person is unhappy almost no matter what. Nothing you can do for them will make them happy.

Perhaps happiness is, as Earl Nightingale said, the progressive realization of a worthy ideal.

If Joshua's little bean tree was capable of experiencing happiness in a tree-like way I think it would be happiest when it was reaching for the light – a worthy ideal, slowly but inexorably realized, in ever-greater degrees but never completed.

Do you have a philosophy on life and happiness? How committed are you to this belief? Is it realistic? Is it logical? And most importantly of all, is it helping you?

Whatever your philosophy on happiness; taking responsibility for your growth, having the courage to face life, and get the best out of whatever experiences you face is undoubtedly the best strategy for growth for every aspect of your nature.

I hope in some small way this book can help you in that pursuit by giving you a formula for extracting more of the rich marrow out of life. It works for everyone that works it. Life is a wonderful adventure. You are already very good at it, but you can get better. Every effort you make to develop and grow through your life experiences will inevitably be reflected in your experience of the world.

It certainly is true that we all have experiences, but not all of us stop and think about what we can learn from these experiences. All too often we bang our heads against the same wall without realizing it is our own making. Not only do we not have to bang our head against this wall, but it's not actually there at all.

Wherever you are on your journey, whatever the circumstances of your life, and however you feel about it all at the moment of reading these words, I want to reach out to you and let you know that you are a wonderful human being capable of far more than you ever thought possible. You have more potential than you can even dream of using. You are perfectly imperfect, just like everyone else. You are no better than anyone else and no worse. You are doing great, but you can do better!

...And you should!

All I ask is the chance to prove that money
won't make me happy.
~ Spike Milligan

Action Exercises

What would a dream life look like for you?

If you knew you couldn't fail, what would you go after?

If you were to leave this world right now, would you be content with what you've done here and who you've become?

When it's all over and someone is summing up your life and the kind of person you are, what do you think they would say?

What would you like them to say?

Write out the answers, or think about them, or better yet, discuss them with a loved one.

2

Where are you stuck?

If the highest aim of a captain were to preserve his ship, he would keep it in port forever.

~ *Thomas Aquinas*

My dad was always a hardworking carpenter, so much so he would get on the roof of the house (or on top of any building) to fix whatever was broken. I, on the other hand, am the total opposite of him in relation to his handy work. If you ever saw me with a hammer in my hand you could be sure that I

27

may end up breaking something. I did not inherit the gift being a handyman or carpenter like my other two brothers did.

During my teenager years, I tried to learn as much as I could from my brothers as they were the computer wizards of the house. I fell in love with how the computers worked. My first computer was 8086 and my first program was written in a Commodore 64 computer. From that moment on, my mind was like a sponge. I wanted to learn more and more. My dad could not understand why I would change the color of the monitor every day. One day the computer screen letters were blue, the next day green, and the next red.

It was always an adventure inside and outside of the house. I played outside with my friends, but as soon as it was night time it was my time to play on the computer. What a joy it was to play for hours, learning about what a computer could do. I must say this was in the 1980's, which means pre-Internet days. So...no Google searches or YouTube videos.

During my late teens and young adult days I developed a great desire to learn more and more about how to program the computers and how they worked. Eventually, I came to the point where I got stuck. The computer had so much potential, but because of my current level of awareness I could not use all its power and capacity.

Have you ever felt stuck? How did it feel? Like one of my mentors says, "Being Stuck Stinks." It's ok to feel stuck occasionally. It means we have reached our ceiling. The question is what are we going to do now to get out of this situation? How will we get to the next level? Interestingly when we *feel* stuck, a state of mental immobility, our physical body can also become paralyzed. And until you allow your mind to get unstuck you will not move forward to achieve your purpose in life.

I would like to share a story from a dear friend of mine. His name is Rodrigo and he has a lovely farm house. Throughout the years he and his wife, Susana, have transformed the farm house into a palace. He was telling me a story about when he decided to change the original wood floor to a modern tile floor. Rodrigo's favorite store is Home Depot. All the employees know him because he spends so much time in there. Susana thinks they own every possible tool in Home Depot because Rodrigo spend so much time there.

On one of the trips to Home Depot he brought Susana and asked her to choose which tile she would like for the kitchen floor. As always, Rodrigo convinced her that he was the perfect man for the job!

For three weeks straight Rodrigo was kneeling on the floor working away! Of course, being a self-proclaimed handyman, he did not follow the instructions to wear the suggested knee pads. As he shared the story I could imagine him stubbornly working on the floors. Knee pads are for wimps, right? Wrong! Oh my goodness, by the time the floor was finished his right knee had swelled up considerably and had become very painful to move. He left it to get better on its own.

But it didn't get better.

After a couple of months of rest his knee didn't get better. He finally decided to go to a doctor and got the diagnosis: Housemaid Knee. So, he was sent back home to rest his knee. Rodrigo was stuck. His knee was not getting better. After a year with the pain he decided to go back, but now to a specialist who took x-rays and MRIs...and they told him there was absolutely nothing wrong with his knee!

What? How could that be possible? Rodrigo's brain had decided the fate for the muscles of his leg. He decided he was going to rest his knee and his body complied with it.

With the confirmation from a doctor that there was nothing wrong with his knee—in fact, it was more psychological than physical—Rodrigo's body gradually began to operate normally again. However, the whole process ended up being a three-year journey!

Rodrigo shared with me an interesting detail. He said, "I realize now that I've learned much more in life from my injuries than my health, and that particular injury really hammered home the principle 'use it or lose it!' We are designed to use our marvelous bodies, not to continually seek out inactivity because it's comfortable."

It is true for us and all other life; isn't it? We are designed for continual growth in all areas of our lives and personalities (mind, body, and spirit included).

If we are not growing in a specific area of our life, if we are not getting better, then we are getting worse! Nothing stands still. Everything is moving in one direction or the other. As successful entrepreneur and TV spokesman for Remington Products Victor Kiam said, "Even if you fall on your face, you're still moving forward." We are either going forward or backward. We are in a state of growth or a state of disintegration.

> *Minds grow as they grapple with ideas.*
> *~Fred Smith Sr.*

Fred Smith Sr. asserted that our minds grow as they grapple with ideas. Everything is perpetually changing. Our world around us today is changing at a faster rate than ever before. The only way we can be comfortable in such a world is to learn to learn. Psychologist and Pioneer of Photo Reading Paul Scheele says that in order to release our Natural Genius we must learn to be uncomfortable with the idea that we need to be in a constant journey of learning, unlearning, and relearning to release the Natural Genius that is in each one of us.

We need to be able to constantly adapt and grow. We need to constantly exercise our ability to learn, unlearn, and relearn! I once heard a creative speaker demonstrate this idea. While he was opening his presentation he walked on stage with huge six-foot tall red dinosaur. He set it down on the stage and then wrote "R T C" in big letters on a flip chart. He then took a live white mouse out of his briefcase and let it run from hand to hand for about 30 seconds. Looking up at the audience he asked, "Who would have put money on this little guy outlasting this big guy sixty-five million years ago? Then he turned to the board and said, "Resistant To Change!"

I have studied different communicators, I have my own experience as an international professional speaker, trainer, and coach; but I've never come across another opener like that! It makes a great point, doesn't it?

We are adaptive beings. We can assess and learn from our environments and change to fit them more optimally. In fact, adapting like this is more than just change.

I recently read that: You are always a student, never a master. You have to keep moving forward. In order for us to get unstuck we need to keep on looking forward. And that requires a change in our doing so we can transform ourselves.

Your are always a student, never a master.

You have to keep moving forward.

~Conrad Hall

Remember my story about being stuck? Well, I had to look for help to get unstuck. I did not stop my relentless search and was thus able to go beyond my stuck state and develop a new awareness of the capabilities given to me by our creator.

To thrive for sustained periods of time we need to be in a state of perpetual transformation.

For many people this is difficult to do. We don't like change. As Tom Feltenstein said, "Change is good...You go first!"

The problem with the world is the intelligent people are full of doubts and the stupid people are full of confidence.

~ Charles Bukowski

Action Exercises

Where are you stuck in your life?

Which specific fears are holding you back?

Are there things you want, that you are not going after?

When was the last time you did something you've never done before?

Write out the answers, or think about them, or better yet, discuss them with a loved one.

3

If not you, then who is going to do it?

Responsibility is the price of freedom.
~ Elbert Hubbard

Between stimulus and response there is a space. In that
space is our power to choose our response. In our
response lies our growth and our freedom.
~Viktor E. Frankl

It's funny how we have a feeling of invincibility
when we're young; isn't it? We envision

39

ourselves as our favorite superhero. When I was young I could eat anything I wanted and at any time. Now, as I age gracefully, I look for healthier food alternatives. I still enjoy a good Puerto Rican style fried chicken, but try to limit what I do. If I don't limit, who will do it for me?

I remember going to eat many years ago while working for an International Technology Company in the city of Hato Rey in the beautiful island of Puerto Rico. A group of people decided to go out to eat and we had very hefty meals and a great time. We were having a blast as a team, when suddenly a wife of an executive came by to say hello and ask how I was.

As a team, we served the same faces every day, from secretaries to executives. We made sure all their technology needs were met. I remember Mike saying, "You know more people than I do and I've been here ten years longer. How do you do it?"

That was an interesting thought. How did I get noticed by so many people in that company? I responded with, "I am just being me."

There must be something different. Why do some people connect and others do not? There is a certain dynamic or culture that exists in every organization. If you have been around technology gifted people then you can remember that in many cases anyone that is not gifted like them is looked down on—as if unwelcomed and/or stupid. "Why don't you get it? It is so simple!" they may taunt.

Have you experience this behavior?

As early as when I was studying in the seminary I remember my authoritative figures told us we needed to focus on people to communicate the message. It didn't matter if it was in church or in the office because we are all people. In this situation, I was trying to connect with the people that I served.

A few years later I remembered this when I was coaching someone who really wanted to make an impact and change some of his behaviors. We discussed all the benefits and eventually he took the plunge. He started to make a difference in his community even though other people were not connecting with him at the beginning.

His relationship with those around him changed forever. All those that wanted him to stay the same cut their friendship as soon as he started to improve and change.

It is a peculiar realization when you begin to change and grow that the people around you, many of whom you love and who love you, don't like it!

As we discussed in the last chapter, no one really likes change. We especially do not like change that happens to us, as opposed to change that we choose.

There's a certain dynamic to any club or group and the homeostasis is maintained by everyone doing and being the same. If someone goes and changes, it ruins it for everyone else!

This is especially true of a 'negative' type group: smoking, partying, irresponsible behavior, drug use, etc. If you change your life and stop going to the club every weekend you are reminding your friends at the club that maybe they shouldn't be living like this anymore. Worse yet, you're saying that you have the courage to change and they don't. Now things are awkward and they have a decision to make. They must justify their choice to stay right where they are, and very often they do this by bashing you and your noble attempt at a better life!

"Who do you think you are anyway? So, you're better than us now?"

One time I heard the story of a woman, I will call her Jane. She had been trying to stop smoking for years. She used to go out with her friends at work and one day she had enough. She wanted to quit so she went to her doctor and asked for help. Surprisingly, her doctor advised her against quitting. The doctor actually recommended Jane to carry on smoking! How can you deceive yourself to that extent?

Very easily.

We don't like change. We don't like feeling bad about ourselves, so we will go to ridiculous extents to justify our thoughts, feelings, and actions.

If you are going to change then you have to be ready for everything to change.

What does this mean for our quest for success? It means that if you are going to change then you have to be ready for everything to change. Don't worry, it's a good thing! Be aware in advance though because it hurts when people don't do what you expect them to do.

If you think about this, it means that both people you love and are indifferent to will try to keep you stuck where you are, consciously or often unconsciously, because they don't understand or they don't want change to happen to them.

To put it another way, it means when you decide you want something, you need to overcome the gravitational pull of everyone in your environment because they don't want you to have it! I know that sounds crazy, but it is true. It's not that you can't get them on board, often you can! But, you need to grow and take them with you—not expect them to help you get there. And some of them will accept the new you, but many will not.

Everyone in your life has a vested unconscious desire for you to carry on as you are. So, if you want change, no one is going to do it for you. The international speaker and famous mentor Jim Rohn used to say, "If you want something to change, don't expect it to change. You need to change yourself." We all have to take complete and utter responsibility for ourselves. Expecting others to do it for us, or even to be on board with us, just sets us up for disappointment.

This presents many problems for well-meaning parents, doesn't it? My wife, Cely, and I have many conversations about spoiling the children and the constant evaluation of whether we're neglecting them or empowering them.

My friend and business partner shared a great story with me that demonstrated how to best empower our kids to help them mature and grow. His two boys love the outdoors. They are always on adventures and exploring different mountains or swamps. One night his son received a called from a friend. The friend asked the son if the son could come and help him get unstuck from mud. The son asked what happened and the friend started laughing as he shared the story of where he was and how he got stuck there. After the call the son asked his father for some advice. He wanted to know if he should go or not. If you were a father and heard a story like this, your first response may be asking why he was not calling his parents to get him. Or what would happen if your child got stuck also. This man responded with five wise words, "It's your decision, my boy."

So, the young adventurer decided to go and rescue his friend from the mud pit in the middle of nowhere. After eight hours, his son came back. Based on my friend's description, the son was unrecognizable. His truck was completely covered in mud as was the son. His mom did not allow him in the house and had to use the hose to wash him before she allowed inside.

The important part of this story was not that he went to help his friend. Rather, it is what happened after. The son said to his father, "Thank you for trusting me to do the right thing and by the way, I am not going out off-road again." He learned his lesson and at the same time built up a great connection with his father.

He realized that he could make decisions on his own and that some may be good ones and others may not, but he could make his own decisions.

For as long as you believe that someone or something else is responsible for your growth, nothing is going to change.

Taking responsibility is the first step of many. For as long as you believe that someone or something else is responsible for your growth, nothing is going to change. The world will continue to hold up the same merciless mirror, reflecting the same life experience until you acquiesce and agree to take the helm and chart your own course.

If you are not living your dream life—and most people aren't—it's not your mom's or dad's fault, nor your spouse's, your children's, the government's, the economy's, the weather's, anything's, or anyone else's fault.

We have all been gifted with the ability to choose what to do in any and every moment. Different choices take us in different directions.

But with that marvelous gift of free will comes the responsibility for the decisions we make. In many ways, it's as simple as that!

Years ago, I used to commute into the city of Chicago on the train and underground. It was 90 minutes each way of looking at the same sad faces every day sitting in the same sad seats! As I think about it while writing this chapter it reminds me a scene of the kid's movie *Zootopia*, where a group of business hamsters walk in line and do the same thing over and over and over. To the point that Wilde the fox planned to get the hamsters money by selling them popsicles made of snow. And every one of the hamsters just paid him because the other hamster did the same thing.

When I was telling a colleague at work of my amusing thought, Einstein's quote leapt out at me and smacked me over the head, "Insanity is doing the same things over and over again expecting different results."

I'm sure some of the three million people who commute to Chicago every day are very happy and grateful for the opportunity. However, I'm equally certain that many dream of a bigger, better life. I wonder how many of them will wait until someone does it for them?

Guess how long they'll be waiting? A very long time.

You take your life in your own hands and what happens? A terrible thing, no one to blame!

~ Erica Jong

Action Exercises

Who do you depend on in your life?

What do you depend on them for?

Are there important things in your life that you are waiting for other people do deliver?

What would it take for you to do what you are waiting for them to do?

Write out the answers, or think about them, or better yet, discuss them with a loved one.

4

What is it you want, I mean really want?

Goals that are casually set are freely abandoned at the first obstacle.

~ Zig Ziglar

Setting goals is the first step in turning the invisible into the visible.

~Tony Robbins

While writing this chapter I remembered the story of Jackie. She is a very talented entrepreneur, mother, and wife. She has four kids that are the joy of her life. One day in early December, my friend Jackie arrived back to her home with her youngest son, Jack, who was about three years old at the time. Her house was empty because her husband had taken the other three kids to the movies. Jackie realized that she forgot her house keys on the dining table.

She could see the keys through the window in the dining room and she pondered how she would get in her house. She checked each windows or doors to see if any were open but had no luck.

Then an idea popped in to her head, they had a doggie door! Jackie opened her back-fence door and walked up the stairs of her porch and shouted "EUREKA!" The doggie door was open.

All this while, Jack thought his mom was playing with him and he was having a blast. That gave Jackie an idea. She needed to get the keys on the dining room table but had no way of getting them herself. What if Jack could get them for her? As soon as the idea came to her mind she asked Jack, "Can you do something for mommy?"

Jack said, "Anything mommy."

So, she asked him if he would like to play rescuer like he does sometimes and agreed. She instructed him to go through the door and get keys on the dining table.

As soon as Jack pushed the doggie door he was greeted with a million licks from his best pal, his Boston Terrier Penny. Jack got up and said, "I am on a mission, I, I, I need get the keys for mommy." Off he went to the dining room! After a couple minutes passed Jackie heard some noises. She stuck her head through the doggie door and asked Jack if everything was okay. Jack ran towards his mommy with Penny and, while the dog licked

Jackie, he said the keys were too high and he couldn't do it. She asked that he try one more time because it was really important. She gave words of encouragement and solidified that she knew he could do it. After five minutes passed she tried to see through the window to see if everything was okay. To her surprise, she saw Jack sitting on the floor of the kitchen. As she looked she could see that he was eating. Then she saw the back of the chair. It was next to the sideboard in the kitchen.

Apparently, Jack had given up on his rescue mission and instead dragged the chair into the kitchen. He had put it up against the sideboard, climbed up onto it, and stood on his tiptoes to unhook his brothers' and sister's advent calendars off the wall. There he was, sitting on the floor eating all the chocolates out of them!

While reading this story for the first time I laughed a lot. I've thought about it since then and realized it highlights a really important aspect of human nature. When it comes to someone else's goals almost anything is too much trouble, too difficult, or inconvenient. But when it comes to our own goals there is almost no limit to the risks we'll take, the energy we will invest, and the creativity we can draw upon to satisfy our hearts' desires.

When we are locked onto a goal that's important to us, everything in life is simpler. Decision making is easy. Priorities are sorted in a heartbeat. Distractions don't stand a chance.

What is it that you want? What will stimulate your best thinking today? What will cause you to launch and push onward, even if you haven't had your coffee yet? There's an old saying, "No one washes a rental car!" It's true, isn't it? If you don't own it, you just don't feel the same way about it. Don't let anyone else dictate your goals for you. As Jim Rohn used to say, "If you are not willing to risk the unusual, you will have to settle for the ordinary."

If you are not willing to risk the unusual, you will have to settle for the ordinary.

~Jim Rohn

You must find things that you want to go after! You are worth it. You deserve it and as you progressively grow to the point where you achieve your goals and dreams you will attain more of that seemingly elusive thing called happiness.

Earl Nightingale said, "Happiness is the progressive realization of a worthy ideal." It is a funny thing that most people never really think about. What it is they want? I mean really want. They will list off the things that they don't want very quickly, but seem to get stuck with what they do want.

Paul Martinelli often says, "Most people say they want a lot more than they actually do and they settle for far less than they could easily get."

What are some of the things you truly want? Give yourself permission to stop and think about this question. Don't include the things you need. There is far less motivational drive involved with needs.

Happiness is the progressive realization of a worthy ideal

~ Earl Nightingale

The wisest king in history said, "The plans of the diligent lead to profit as surely as haste leads to poverty." I want you to think of the things that ignite your passion, the things that give you that surge of energy and a feeling of purpose. These are your worthy goals and dreams, and I've got good news for you concerning them. You don't have to settle for a life that excludes them. You just have to pinpoint what they actually are.

I think one of the main benefits of being clear on this is that the desire to achieve or attain something is the rocket fuel that pushes us forward. It tempts us into growth. Going after something we don't actually know how to achieve (because we haven't paved the way yet) forces us to tackle new situations and challenges in order to continue the process of growth in our lives. Napoleon Hill in this timeless masterpiece *Think and Grow Rich* asserts, "You need to have a burning desire in order to go after your dreams."

It forces us to take advantage of opportunities that we didn't see before or discounted as too risky. Going after something we want forces us to pick ourselves up after things go wrong and to try something else. Indifference does none of these things.

The things that we want can be large or small. They can take a few hours to achieve or a lifetime. The bigger the goal and the longer it takes to achieve, the more order it introduces into our lives.

Order is heaven's first law. "In the beginning God created the heaven and the earth..." You and I have a purpose why we exist and we were put on this planet. In order to achieve it we must know what it is we want.

For us to achieve anything meaningful, we need order and movement. One without the other doesn't really work, does it?

In James Allen's great book, *As a Man Thinketh,* there is a chapter about thought and purpose. At the beginning of this chapter, he reminds us, "Until thought is linked with purpose, there is no intelligent accomplishment."

Until thought is linked with purpose,
there is no intelligent accomplishment
~James Allen

So, the order that comes from a clear objective permeates every aspect of our life. It brings order to our thinking. It brings order to our actions. It brings order to our results.

When I talk to people about this, most of them can quickly see that order comes from a clear direction, objective, or compass bearing. What they truly struggle with is the answer to life's greatest question: What is my purpose?

Peter Drucker said something marvelous to assist with the answer, "Only musicians, mathematicians, and a few early maturing people, their numbers limited, know what they want to do from an early age. The rest of us have to find out."

As you embark on this journey of 'finding out' your life purpose, you're going to have to push past a lot of things that hold most people back from this journey.

Fear will try to creep in and tell you, "Oh, those are just pipe-dreams. You need to be grateful for what you have."

Only musicians, mathematicians and a few early maturing people, their numbers limited, know what they want to do from an early age. The rest of us have to find out.

~Peter Drucker

"Not everyone is marked for greatness. Just stay where you are. Do what has the least amount of risk." Essentially, all of these fear-based thoughts are attempting to convince you to settle for a life that is far less than you are capable of being. Is that what you want? Of course not, remember fear is nothing more than False Evidence Appearing Real. So, feed your faith and starve your fear.

Then you're going to have to learn to face your fears. They will always be there. They'll be waiting for your weakest moments so they can swoop in and tell you to give up. But when you're willing to pull the mask off of fear, you'll see that all the things you are tempted to worry about are ridiculous.

Remember fear is nothing more than False Evidence Appearing Real, so feed your faith and starve your fear.

Yes, you might fall down. You might look foolish. You might make a huge mistake. But the other side of that looks like this:

- You'll get back up.
- You'll learn from mistakes.
- You'll become an inspiration to others.

If I am given an option it is worth the trials, the mistakes, the obstacles, and even the temporary foolish moment. Peter Drucker also said, "People who don't take risks generally make about two big mistakes a year. People who do take risks make about two big mistakes a year." I'd rather make my mistakes actively engaging in the pursuit of my goals and dreams. How about you?

The problem with quoting people off the Internet is you can never actually be sure they said it.

~ Abraham Lincoln

Action Exercises

When was the last time you sat down and listed all the things you want?

What are the five most important things you would like to achieve?

Which areas of your life are you really content with?

Which areas of your life are you not content with?

Write out the answers, or think about them, or better yet, discuss them with a loved one.

5

What is real, the danger or the fear?

*We cannot live better than in seeking
to become better.*

~ *Socrates*

I remember sitting in a restaurant eating with my family. My little boy, Joshua, was learning to walk. He wanted to explore and try to walk everywhere. He was about one year old and any moving thing caught his attention. The owner of the restaurant knew how wonderful it was to have a glimpse of technology all around including in the floor. He installed thick glass windows in the floor and you could see televisions and other things in each of these windows. As Joshua stumbled while walking towards the window in the floor an interesting thing happened. He would look at the glass door but would not want to go over it or step on it. I never understood why.

Later on in life Joshua learned how to go over the window and even jump on it. But every time that something new appeared he had a similar approach. One day I was in a mastermind and coaching session with one of my mentors and he shared a similar experience with his daughter.

During one of our sessions he shared something that was very interesting. While he was studying Cognitive Behavior in London he was examining the 'fears' babies are born with. According to research, there were just two responses: a fear response to loud noises and a fear response to the threat of falling. This caught my attention.

He continue and had quoted a research study that used glass floors over a ground that visibly dropped away sharply under the glass to see if the babies avoided crawling out over the dropping floor.

As I heard this my mind transported me back to that day in the restaurant. Was that the reason Joshua did not want to walk over the glass door in the floor? It would not be until later in life that I would understand why babies and each us react the way we do.

It has been very interesting and thought provoking to study the mind, personal development, and the brain; all while having a child. Watching his development and wondering why he leaned toward certain behaviors, testing theories, and then wondering how he will react has given me a great opportunity to study growth and development.

The idea that we are born with just two fears is very interesting to me. It provides a great deal of hope for the future of anyone who has suffered trauma that gets in the way of living their life and achieving the things they want to achieve.

The developmental stages and the fears the children learn as they develop are also very interesting.

At around eight to ten months, babies begin to understand 'object permanence.' Before this point, if something is in their awareness it exists. When it is removed from their awareness it ceases to exist. But after this stage, the idea that something is still in existence but just not there at that moment occurs. This leads to other trains of thought, like, "Where has mommy gone? When will she be back?" This is connected to separation anxiety.

I had to go oversees for a business trip to England, Spain and Germany. It started as a twenty-one-day trip. Before I left for the trip Joshua was happy and calm. He would ask where I was if I was not around, but he knew I was in my office. After I left for my trip he asked where I was and when would I be back. This progressed to Joshua asking where I was several times a day for the remainder of my trip.

At my returned, Joshua immediately latched onto me and has never let me go! Our relationship was forever changed after that trip.

One of the other key developmental stages for children occurs with the development of the imagination. Every parent notices a difference in the play of their child if they pay attention. They start making stuff up. They start lying! What is interesting about this stage is that fears can then come from sources that can't be seen. Enter bogey men, the monster under the bed, and things that go bump in the night!

We were spending some time in Puerto Rico during summer. It was a beautiful day sunny, the beaches were warm, and we had a great day. Right after finishing our dinner we decided to go back to our hotel where every night we got into the pool before going to bed. In our way back to it a massive tropical storm came through the top part of the island. It was not a surprise for me but it was Joshua's first time. The storm was pouring down like there was no tomorrow. When we got to the hotel garage every spot was full. The only available spots were in the outside level of the garage.

At the beginning I looked at Joshua's face and he looked scared. He was trying to process the experience. It was something new for him and he looked at me. He saw that I was calm in that situation. He was learning in that moment not to fear that experience. We ran to the hotel and then we watched the majestic thunder and lightning show through the window of our hotel floor.

It is a normal part of children's development to go through these different stages of fear. What is important is that they are transitory. As children learn to overcome these fears they learn that they can deal with life, they can overcome challenges, and say to themselves: 'That wasn't so bad after all!' As adults, though, if we are stuck with a certain irrational fear, it may or may not be a problem. If it is stopping us from getting what we want, then maybe it is a problem to be worked on and overcome.

It's an interesting thing about fear; we put total faith in it. We feel that something is going to happen and we then trust that implicitly. We allow it to control our thinking, our feeling, our actions, and therefore our results.

Perhaps this is what Roosevelt was talking about in his inaugural address when he said:

The only thing we have to fear is fear itself.

If you think about it, it's interesting because the fear we experience doesn't exist anywhere in the entire universe except inside of us. You can't point to it anywhere in the world other than the feelings, thinking, actions, and sometimes even the symptoms you experience in your body.

So does that mean fear isn't real? If two people face the same situation, one feels fear and the other doesn't, does that mean that one of them is making it up?

Fear is not to be confused with danger. Make no mistake, danger is real. Busy roads are dangerous and cars can kill you. They can kill you if you step out into the road. If you are in the road and there is a car coming for you, you should get out of the way quickly! In the right situation, panic can even be a very appropriate emotion. But that's very different from sitting safely in your house panicking because of the cars out on the road. Experiencing a fear of cars when you are safe inside is an irrational fear. It's not real.

It sounds like a silly statement, but that's what we do when we fear fear. With healthy concern, sensible caution, and a few basic safety procedures there is no need for the emotional response at all. Why use it then? Because we've learned to use it and now the tail is wagging the dog!

If you think about it, if fear is successful in its objective, you avoid the situation you fear and never actually know if the fear was founded in the first place. And because you always experience the fear, you never find out what would happen if you just exercised basic caution without the emotion. The emotion will convince you of its necessity and if you comply, you'll never know any different. Every time you engage avoidance because of fear, you are reinforcing the credibility of the fear.

The interesting thing about the body's response to fear is that it is exactly the same for an imagined fear as it is for an actual fear of something right in front of you in the material world.

If you are in the African Savanna and you see a lion, your body responds the same whether you actually see a lion or whether you just thought you saw a lion.

If you just think about that, it is amazing. Imagine you are sitting at home staring blankly out the window. Suddenly just a single thought can pop into your head. Depending on the thought, a feeling of sadness or euphoria or lustfulness or anger can sweep through your body in an instant. Your pancreas secretes a hormone and your liver makes an enzyme that wasn't there just moments before. The blood flow around your body is altered.

What was the cause of all these physiological changes? A single thought in your mind that doesn't exist anywhere except right there and only then for a fleeting second.

Bruce Lipton talks about the effects of fear on the body and its ability to perform in a state of stress in his series on Conscious Parenting. He discusses the three key things that happen when we are in a state of fear.

First, the cells of the body move from growth into protection. Blood moves from the viscera at the core of the body out to the extremities (muscles of the arms and legs) in order to engage in fight or flight.

Second, the immune system shuts down because there is no point using energy fighting a virus that may kill you in ten days if this lion could eat you in the next ten seconds.

And third, the blood moves away from the fore brain to the hind brain so that instead of reason and logic you are better able to engage in reflexive behaviors. You lose your ability to think rationally when you are stressed.

Estimates put the figure at well over 90% for the things we fear but never actually happen. I once heard worry described as chewing gum for the mind – it just gives it something to do but produces no meaningful results.

If a fear of loud noises or a fear of falling is holding you back from reaching your dreams, then you can take comfort in the fact that they've been there all along. But if it's a fear of anything else, then that's something you've picked up along the way. It's something you've learned to see in a certain way and that means it's something you can unlearn and relearn in a more helpful and healthy way.

Put another way, there are beliefs about the world that you have acquired throughout your life. These beliefs are responsible for the emotions you experience in your body in response to events in the outside world (and your inside world). The feelings you experience in that marvelous body of yours—like doubt, fear, and anxiety—stop you from doing things that you would otherwise like to do. If any of these things are stopping you from achieving your goals and dreams, then the underlying beliefs that are responsible need to go!

I learned that courage was not the absence of fear, but the triumph over it. The brave man is not he who does not feel afraid, but he who conquers that fear.

~ Nelson Mandela

Action Exercises

What are you most afraid of?

What are four other things that you are afraid of?

Are any of these five fears holding you back from what you want to achieve?

What would change in your life if you could overcome one or more of these fears?

Write out the answers, or think about them, or better yet, discuss them with a loved one.

6

Does everyone see it that way?

Men are disturbed not by the things that happen to them, but by the views they take of them.

~ Epictetus

It's not what you look at that matters, it's what you see.

~Henry David Thoreau

One of the most empowering exercises I have ever been a part of was called the One Hundred People Technique. It is a simple exercise, but extremely powerful.

I was part of a weekend training course called TurningPoint and one of the exercises asked us to think about an issue that may have affected us in the past. I was working on an issue that I brought to mind with my partner as part of a weekend training course. First of all, I described the problem with a few details and described the emotion I experienced when faced with this problem. My partner then asked me to imagine one hundred people, very similar to myself, who were facing the same challenge. "Would they all respond in the same way as you?" she asked.

I thought about the question very briefly and said, "Yes. Of course, they would, because that's the proper response to this type of challenge. Everyone would respond the same way, wouldn't they?"

She answered with another question, "Well, what might some of the other possible ways of responding be?"

Eventually, and somewhat reluctantly, I said that some people may be even angrier and more offended than I was.

She said, "Good! And what about some of the others?"

"Well, I guess some others might not be really bothered by this sort of thing."

"Good!" she said again, "What about some other responses?"

After a few minutes of this I came up with many different possible responses: angered, laughter, indifference, offended, pleased, scornful, sarcastic, guilty, etc.

She said, "And do you really believe that some people may respond in these different ways?"

And I genuinely believed that they could.

Then she said, "Well, can you see then, that if it is possible for different people to respond in different ways to the same event, it can't be the event that is responsible for the feeling. It must be something else. It must be the individual!"

It was a critical point for me because not only did I really accept for the first time that it was something in me that was creating the emotions, but I also realized that I only got to that realization by actually doing the exercise.

We are disturbed, not by the events of life, but by the views we take of them. ~ Epictetus

You see, I had heard the exercise explained by the lecturer before we split up into pairs. And I understood it, but I didn't really get it. It was only when I took part in the exercise and actually came face to face with what I believed at a subconscious level that I realized it was what was inside of me that was causing the problem, not something outside of me. It wasn't them at all. It was me.

It is a powerful realization indeed when you understand that your beliefs are the key to your emotions. It is what you believe about the event that causes the emotion, not the event itself.

The way you see the world also comes from what you believe. Your perception of the world is a consequence of your acquired beliefs. And your beliefs are the result of a learning process, not a reflection of reality.

Some people see a situation a certain way and they feel they only have one real option of how to precede. As a result of this belief, they keep banging their head against the same wall, over and over again, going round and round in circles, getting the same results.

Other people see the same situation differently. They perceive a number of different options. They make different choices and they never experience the same challenges that the other person is stuck with.

Choice is a function of awareness.

~ Michael Beckwithg

One evening at a dinner in Paraguay, I had the distinct pleasure of sitting with an amazing group of leaders. One of the many brilliant things shared during one of the transformational leadership sessions was that choice is a function of awareness. The speaker said, 'We are crockpots and until you are not aware of it you will still see things in the same way."

His words impacted me and made me understand something very important. The more aware you are, the more options you perceive in any given situation. The more options you are aware of, the higher the likelihood of picking the best option for you in that particular set of circumstances.

This is especially true in relationships. If you allow yourself to continually respond in the same way because you think you are right, then it can perpetuate the same vicious disagreements. You go round and round in angry circles, sometimes for years.

It is not uncommon for people to cling to their sense of rightness, even long after the other party has passed away. The same emotions of anger or resentment rise up at the mere thought of the disagreement.

If you can find another way of seeing this —if you can search for other ways to respond—

93

you will eventually bring about a different, better, healthier end result.

And while it may be true that the obligation sits equally with both parties in the relationship, if one just cannot see things differently at this time, and the other can, then the one with the greater awareness has the responsibility for moving things forward. There is a lovely scene in the movie *Night at the Museum* when Ben Stiller's character is hitting the monkey in the face and the monkey is hitting him back. On and on it goes for some time. Up rides Teddy Roosevelt on his horse and says, "Larry, why are you hitting the monkey?" He says, "He started it!" And Teddy replies, "Larry, who's evolved?"

The responsibility sits with the person with the higher awareness.

Men are anxious to improve their
circumstances, but are unwilling to improve
themselves; they therefore remain bound.
~James Allen

James Allen was British Author from the late 19th century. He was the creator of *The Herald of the Golder Age,* a publication where he helped countless number of people to understand how their thinking will impact everything they do. His most famous masterpiece *As a Man Thinketh* was based on the Biblical text from the book of Proverbs 23:7 "As a man Thinketh in his heart, so is he." His quote reads, "Men as anxious to improve their circumstances, but are unwilling to improve themselves, they therefore remain bound." Shows us how many times we see things but never do anything because we lack awareness.

Paul Martinelli was one of the first people I heard talking about the idea of awareness. The more I think about it, the more I think it is the answer to everything.

So how do we gain a higher level of awareness? Experience. However, it is not simply by experience. Everyone gets experience, but not everyone grows at the same rate; do they? The experience must be evaluated in some way and insight needs to be harvested from the experience. That insight needs to lead to change in the way we see the world and how we operate in it.

So, you could say that intention mixed with continually evaluated experience leads to a greater level of awareness over time.

If I had a dollar for every time I got distracted man I'd love some ice cream right now.

~ Unknown

Action Exercises

What is holding you back from taking the next step toward your goal or your dream?

What other options can you identify rather than not moving forward?

Write out five different actions you could take, irrespective of whether or not you think they will work?

Is there anyone you know who could deal with this differently? If so, what would they do?

Write out the answers, or think about them, or better yet, discuss them with a loved one.

7

Are you milking this?

Every action has its pleasures and its price.

~ Socrates

Do not go where the path may lead, go instead where there is no path and leave a trail.

~ Ralph Waldo Emerson

As a kid, I remember listening to my mother talking about different historic characters. She was an amazing history teacher. One of the characters that she mentioned was Nelson Mandela. As a kid and teen I study some his story in school, but it was not until my adult years that I understood what he really did for his country and his people. It was amazing how he never focused on his lack of freedom or issues. He focused on what he could do for his people and how he could make a positive change. But it was not easy. He spent twenty-seven years in prison. After he was released from prison he could have complained and become bitter, but he used it as an opportunity to continue his work.

He is an inspiration to so many and in 1993 he received the Novel Peace Price for his efforts to bring equality in South Africa.

How many times do we just try to milk a situation because it looks bad or because it may benefit us?

Susan Galbraith once said: "Once you stop worrying about what you haven't got, you can start enjoying what you have."

Why didn't we spend time enjoying what we had? Well, certainly part of it had to do with adjusting to a new reality from the position of our expectations. And that takes time.

Then there's another aspect to it. I call it the 'poor me' syndrome. This syndrome occurs during the moment when we first realize there is a definite benefit to sharing the story of how unfortunate we have been in order to receive attention and sympathy. Being a victim can have good payoffs, after all. It also excuses you from the effort of trying, doesn't it?

Life is 10% what happens to you and 90%
how you react to it.

~ Charles R. Swindoll

Author, educator, and pastor Charles R. Swindoll said: "Life is 10% what happens to you and 90% how you react to it." That is so true. When something happens to you it is your choice how you react, not the other way around. You can decide to react in a positive or in a negative way.

We have the choice on how we communicate our situations to others. Sometimes we share the good, other times we share the bad. Nevertheless, it must be acknowledged that there are often benefits to us in our proclaimed misery.

I remember studying how the brain works during a week-long seminar. The lecturer gave an example of one of her clients who was being treated for migraines and other concerns. She asked the client, "What happens when you get one of your headaches?"

She explained the awful experience, "Well, I have to go to bed and shut the curtains because I need absolute quiet. My husband has to come home early and feed the kids. He has to do their homework with them, make dinner, bathe them, and put them to bed. I'm unable to help in any way because I have to lie down and rest."

While I certainly don't want to offend people who suffer with migraines or any other type of similar conditions, is it possible that there are significant secondary gains with many of our complaints?

While in training session, one of the presenters said something very interesting. Whenever anyone first explains their problems to him, the very first question he asks himself is: how convenient is this? In other words, what are you getting out of this?

Dr. David Hawkins recommended putting a sign up on the mirror where you could see it every morning that reads "Yours is the saddest story I've ever heard!"

There are two types of people in the world, aren't there? There are life giving people and life draining people. Life giving people add value. They leave you a little bit better than you were when they found you. They tend to see the world from your perspective with you. We don't seduce people by telling them how great we are; we seduce them by telling them how great they are.

You may have heard the story of the lady who went to dinner with Mr. Gladstone one evening and Mr. Disraeli the next, both prominent English Statesman. She said, "After dinner with Mr. Gladstone I thought he was the smartest person in England; but after dinner with Mr. Disraeli I thought I was!" What a difference between the two! Life giving people make you feel better about yourself, but they also make you feel better about the world and everyone in it. They seem to lift everything and leave you with hope. You always feel better leaving the company of a life-giving person.

Life draining people, on the other hand, tend to talk about themselves and they see the world from their perspective. You always feel worse when leaving the company of life draining people!

Most of us are not aware of our real motivations. A wealthy person can work hard, make money, and declare that she is doing it for the family. Yet, the family never sees her and when they do she seems angry. They then feel like they can't live up to her high expectations. They feel like a disappointment to her. Is she really doing it for the family? Is it possible there are hidden motives? She loves the attention and the respect. Maybe she enjoys not having to look after her own children.

On the other side of the coin, a person could be without a job or proper finances and be forced to live on state benefits. This includes suffering at home all day, not enough money for a fancy car, or expensive clothes, or holidays to exotic places. But how convenient could that be?

If you don't have a job, you don't have to go in every day!

Of course, these are simple examples not meant to be illustrative of EVERYONE in those situations, but it is certainly true that the truth is seldom in the appearance of things. In order to move up and move on, we have to let go. If you are going to be mentally and emotionally healthy, you need to let go of the opportunities you have to continually seek pity and sympathy from everyone you meet! If you really want to have a great family life, you need to make it a priority and stop doing all the other things that prevent you from sharing experiences and making memories with your family. If you really want a job, you need to let go of all the upsides of not working and spend your time learning how to become a better job candidate.

Some of you, as you read through this chapter, will be offended at the mere suggestion that your misery has any upside whatsoever. How horrible of me to even come up with such an outlandish idea! Then you will seek out people to validate your feelings. You'll tell them how offended you are. And you will explain again just how awful your lot in life is. Once again, you will soak up whatever sympathy is available. Paul Martinelli describes the tendency of people to look for opportunities to be offended as one of the 'four pillars of drama' in his incredible teachings. Why would anyone possibly look to be offended? Simply because there is something in it for them.

Know thyself. The unexamined life
is not worth living

~ *Socrates*

Perhaps this is why Socrates said 'know thyself.' The unexamined life is not worth living. If you are really honest with yourself, how convenient are your challenges?

Are you prepared to give up these conveniences in order to move forward with your life?

Try to leave out the bit readers tend to skip!

~ Elmore Leonard

Action Exercises

Where are you stuck in your life?

Are there any upsides to being stuck?

What would someone who knows you well say is the reason you are not moving on?

Do you know anyone who is stuck in a key area of their life, who do you know that has significant advantages from staying stuck?

Write out the answers, or think about them, or better yet, discuss them with a loved one.

8

You are perfect just as you are?

Happiness can exist only in acceptance.

~ George Orwell

I was blessed to be part of an elite group of over 250 John Maxwell Team coaches invited by the president of Paraguay to bring leadership transformation to his beautiful country. In my life I have been very fortunate to have opportunities to travel extensively while working with people from over 100 different countries. One of the things that has become so obvious to me is this beautiful paradox:

An investment in knowledge pays the best interest. ~ Benjamin Franklin

Everyone is different and still somehow everyone is the same! One of the United States forefathers, Benjamin Franklin, once said, "an investment in knowledge pays the best interest."

The only good is knowledge and the only evil is ignorance. ~ Socrates

I believe we are all perfectly imperfect children of God. No matter where you go or who you speak to, everyone is stepping forward courageously to face the human condition. One of my mentors said, "Having the courage to say yes to life is an incredible thing." Examples include: the courage of a mother to risk her life to give birth to another life, the courage of a father to stand up as a soldier, the courage of every single one of us to stand up and say yes to our life experiences.

We are not all meant to be star quarterbacks, nor beauty pageant queens. We are not all meant to be presidents or Mother Teresa's. Every single one of us is different. Every single one of us is perfect. Every single one of us struggles in some area of life and every single one of us is loved unconditionally.

If you look around, you see people doing their best. Everyone is doing the best they can. Socrates said man always chooses the good. Man can only choose the good. His only error is that he does not know what is for his own good. Everyone makes the best decision they can at the time.

This simple message has been said time and time again throughout history, "The only sin is ignorance."

If we accept the fact that we do what we do because we don't know better then our path becomes pretty straight forward, doesn't it? How can we learn more and grow more so that we can make better decisions? How can we be just a little more enlightened?

Paul Martinelli often says, "The perfect curriculum for your growth is whatever lies in front of you right now." I find this a very empowering train of thought.

We are all perfectly imperfect. We are God's masterpieces. This is important: you and I are masterpieces.

No one is any better than anyone else. No one is any worse than anyone else. We are all doing the best we can.

However, we can all do better. We all have the opportunity to learn and grow. As we learn and grow we make better decisions. As we make better decisions our life improves.

The realization that we are all merely doing the best we can with what we have certainly makes pride seem empty and forgiveness more of a rational decision. "Forgive us our trespasses as we forgive those that trespass against us," the Lord's Prayer reads. We are all in it together and we are all connected.

There is a story about the word Ubuntu, which, to a certain African tribe means, "I am what I am because of who we all are." It is nice to think that we are ALL doing something because we are connected and part of a bigger family or purpose.

It is said that an anthropologist who was studying the customs and lifestyle of this tribe spent a lot of time with the children. One particular day he decided to play a game with them. He knew they loved candy, so he made a trip to a neighboring town to buy some. He arranged quite a few pieces in a decorative basket and placed the prize at the base of a tree.

Excitedly, he called all the children together explaining that they were going to play a game and the winner would receive the prize, "When I shout 'now', everyone will run as fast as you can to the tree! The first one there wins the entire basket of candy."

Eager to participate, the children lined up and waited for the shout. As soon as the anthropologist yelled, "Now!" all the children grabbed each other by the hand and began running as fast as they could toward the tree. Arriving at exactly the same time, they divided the candy and began to enjoy their prize.

Slightly stunned, the anthropologist asked why they chose to all run together when the winner would have had all the candy to themselves.

"Ubuntu. How could one of us be happy when the others are sad?"

This philosophy and way of life speaks about our interconnectedness. You can't exist as a human all by yourself. Our choices affect others. Every day we have crossroads and decisions. With each decision we either choose to add value to another human life or to take it away. We are always choosing one or the other. Even the decision to do nothing is still a decision.

Part of walking in awareness understands that we are responsible for the condition we leave others in. How has their encounter with us affected them? What lasting impression have we left?

We often talk about leaving a legacy for future generations. Usually, we are referring to finances or inheritance, but what about our daily legacy?

We are building a memorial to ourselves with every sentence, every text message, every email, and every glance.

Realizing this certainly changes our perspective. Doesn't it?

Failure comes only when we forget our ideals and objectives and principles

~Jawaharlal Nehru

Action Exercises

What aspects of you are you not happy with? How do they affect your life?

Do you know anyone who has similar things that is not bothered by them at all or uses them as an advantage?

How could it be true that your weaknesses are also your sensitivities?

Write out the answers, or think about them, or better yet, discuss them with a loved one.

9

Love all life, including yourself!

There are two basic motivating forces; fear and love. When we are afraid, we pull back from life. When we love, we open to all that life has to offer with passion, excitement, and acceptance. We need to learn to love ourselves first, in all our glory and imperfections. If we cannot love ourselves, we cannot fully open our ability to love others or our potential to create.

~ John Lennon

You have flaws. I have flaws. We are not perfect. We're all going to make mistakes. It's simply part of the human process.

Shocking isn't it?

While in the movie Rocky, Silvester Stallone says, "I dunno, she's got gaps, I got gaps, together we fill gaps."

Actually, I'm quite certain you didn't flinch at all when you read those words. Isn't it amazing that although we are fully aware of the fact that mistakes, detours, and unexpected results are part of the process we often allow the fear of their arrival to stall our progress? Some of us get stuck for days or weeks. Still, others struggle with the fear of failure to such a degree that it can derail their dreams indefinitely.

But why? Why do we get stuck?

In the closing chapters of *Think and Grow Rich*, Napoleon Hill uncovers the six basic fears that prevent us from attaining freedom and success:

- The fear of poverty.
- The fear of criticism.
- The fear of ill health.
- The fear of losing someone.
- The fear of old age.
- The fear of death.

Yes, these are basic (or core) fears. However, as we talked about earlier these fears are learned. Depending on how we were raised or what we've experienced, these fears can affect us to a greater or lesser degree.

How do we combat fear? How do we push past the irrational and negative thought patterns that trigger survival mode and constrict the hope around us?

How do we live struggle free?

John C. Maxwell says, "Feed your Faith and starve your fears."

The good news here is that there is a way to retrain your brain. It doesn't matter if you're eighteen or eighty, the negative thoughts that run through your brain can be recognized, rejected, and replaced.

Fear is false evidence appearing real. So if it is false appears real, but is not, then we can remove it and change it.

Let's take a look at how that's accomplished:

Fear is connected to our lens. It has to do with how we see things and especially how we see ourselves. For the most part, we see situations through our own filter or according to certain expectations. We do this automatically. For example, let's say five or six of us were discussing real estate investing during dinner...

The deeper a few of us got into the conversation, the more you checked-out and disengaged.

Why? Because you're not an investor. Not only do you not invest in real estate, but you've never owned a home in your life. In fact, your parents never owned a home either. So, instead of leaning in (which would be alignment), you might choose to lean away. It probably wasn't even a conscious decision. You see, the left side of our brain (the part that's linear and rational) is constantly taking information from our experiences and connecting this information to our current reality in order to project probable outcomes.

So, if the entire table is talking about investing and you don't believe that's something attainable for you, it's likely the left side of your brain made the probable assumption that you'll never need this information and it was harmless to check-out. Hold it right there!

What if investing becomes somehow connected to your future success? What if you're a late bloomer but buying property is now vital to your life? Well, once you have this awareness (become awake to this truth) you have the power to change, to learn, to grow.

Fear robs us of our power.

Maybe you'll have to overcome some of the core fears Napoleon Hill discussed. Fear robs us of our power. While we are saying yes to our dreams and goals, fear is saying no.

Instead of allowing these fears to run around in our brain like a wild banshee, it's up to us to use the power of the 3R's.

- RECOGNIZE them
- REJECT them
- REPLACE them

It's like being the protector of your own brain. If there are negative thoughts and limiting belief systems it's our job to kick them out.

James Allen asserted, "A man's mind may be likened to a garden, which may be intelligently cultivated or allowed to run wild; but whether cultivated or neglected, it must, and will, bring forth. If no useful seeds are put into it, then an abundance of useless weed seeds will fall therein, and will continue to produce their kind."

Let's go one level deeper and talk about how we kick negative thoughts out. It's certainly not by using willpower and choosing not to think negative thoughts. If you've ever attempted to not think about something, you know how well that works.

If you've never tried it, go ahead and spend the next thirty seconds trying not to picture a purple zebra. Don't do it! No purple zebras! Let me guess, they're galloping around in your brain at full speed, right? I thought so.

Instead of attempting to not think negatively, the key is to replace fear and negative thoughts. We do this by reminding ourselves of who we are, what we're made of, and what's available to us.

You can use any positive affirmations you choose. The only requirement is that you believe what you're reading or declaring over yourself.

Simple Bible Scriptures can be very useful. They can act as your Daily Promises. Here are a few: "Everything I put my hand to will prosper." —Psalm 1:3

"I am fully equipped and limitlessly resourced for everything I will face today." —Hebrews 13:21

"I won't drift off my course, because the Word promises I will hear a voice behind me saying, 'This is the direction to walk." —Isaiah 30:21

These are just a few, but you get the point. Replace the lies fear is trying to tell you with the truth of who you really are! When your thought-life is centered on faith and truth you become a living and breathing container of hope. You actually begin to operate on a higher level. You begin to attract the things you desire because you aren't allowing any interference from fear!

I believe it's possible to form the habit of walking free from fear. It may take some practice, but the ability to boldly embrace who we are and live an authentic and courageous life is possible. Remember, failure isn't fatal, and it certainly isn't final.

In his wonderful book, *Sometimes you Win Sometimes you Learn*, John C. Maxwell shares that loosing hurts but if we learn from our failures you can use them to your advantage. Your attitude will be the catalyst to kick fear away in your failure and maintain a teachable attitude towards life.

Up to 85 percent of success in life is due to attitude, while only 15 percent is due to ability.
~John C. Maxwell

So go ahead and try! Whether you fail or not, at least you are busy with living instead of standing on the side-lines of life. That's something to be applauded!

In 2012, Sara Blakely became the youngest self-made billionaire. She was 41. She is the creator and founder of Spanx, a women's apparel product. The thing that impressed me most about her story was her recollection of sitting around the dinner table with her father every evening. He taught her the power of failing big, and failing often. "Every evening he would ask me, 'So, what did you fail at today?' And if there were no failures, Dad would be disappointed."

Lack of failure means you are not stretching yourself outside your comfort zone.

By focusing on failing often, and using it as a freeing and liberating exercise in the process of becoming, Sara was allowed to understand that a lack of failure actually signified that she was not stretching herself far enough out of her comfort zone.

Each day we should strive to fully embrace life and all the mess that it may bring. When we live to be more than we were yesterday, and chase after it without fear, we can begin to discover what we are made of and what we can become!

I encourage you to take risks and push against the imaginary barriers of life. Swim in the deep end! Choose to free fall! Don't worry about failing. If you fail, it's really okay! You'll get up. You'll try again! You'll make it!

It took me 15 years to work out I had no talent for writing, but I couldn't give it up because by then I was too famous.

~ Robert Benchley

Action Exercises

Who do you need to forgive?

Why don't you forgive them?

Where have you made mistakes in your own life?

Why is it so hard for you to forgive yourself?

What would it feel like to genuinely forgive yourself?

Write out the answers, or think about them, or better yet, discuss them with a loved one.

10

If it's worth having it's hard to get!

I can sum up the success of my life in seven words. Never give up. Never, never give up.

~ Winston Churchill

Success is the result of perfection, hard work, learning from failure, loyalty, and persistence.

~ Colin Powell

The spark is fun, isn't it? It's that moment of creation when you give permission to a dream or a goal. That spark is usually accompanied by feelings of determination, optimism, passion, and motivation.

Beginnings are exciting and energizing. They have the freshness of a blank page, and for most people a new endeavor can be almost intoxicating. It's kind of like the honeymoon phase of a relationship. And just like romantic relationships, substance isn't built in the beginning. It's during the trials and the day-to-day encounters with each other that who we are inside is established. It's when we are faced with difficult choices, challenges, trials, and frustrations that we become.

During this process of becoming, our dreams are either being fulfilled or forgotten one choice at a time. It is the process that builds us into who we really are.

Success is developed daily, not in a day.

Look around at your life. Think about your relationships, finances, and career. Now go deeper. Think about the things you're proud of, the things you've settled for, the things you'd like to change.

Everything around you is a manifestation of your daily choices. You are in current active possession of the kingdom you've created for yourself. Good or bad. Like it or not, you are the product of your choices.

The more I meditate on this, the more I realize that there is an art to living out our passion. It is an ebb and flow, a process of constant evolving and adapting.

If you aren't happy with what you currently have, the answer then is to begin to lean in to the choices that say yes to the fulfillment of your dreams and goals. In order to accomplish this there is a leveling of pride that takes place. In order to grow and become all you can be, you need to first take responsibility for who and WHERE you are.

Nothing good was ever born out of excuses

Nothing good was ever born out of excuses, so if you've ever said things like, "This is how I was raised" or "I can't help it, I'm just doing what I know" I want to challenge you to absolutely ban these excuses from your life. You don't have to remain comfortable with terrible circumstances. You can take the sign off of your bathroom mirror because yours doesn't have to be the saddest story ever, but it's up to you to make that decision. Living your best life is your own choice.

It is one of the most liberating things you will ever do. To stand on the wreckage heap of your own broken promises, unfulfilled commitments, lies, masks, failures, and mistakes while placing your signature of ownership on the whole mess is huge. It gives you a starting point, a place of accountability where you can say, "Yes, I'm responsible for all of that, and now I'm going to be responsible for all of this!"

Doing that is better than skydiving for the first time. It's risky, dangerous, wildly vulnerable, and 100% necessary if things are ever going to be any different in your life. Best of all, it's empowering.

We are who we choose to be. Every day. Every moment. We don't have to wait until church on Sunday or even tomorrow morning. We literally have the power to walk in foolishness one minute and turn our entire life around the next. As soon as we realize we are doing something that's not in alignment with our best life, we have the power to choose to turn around. That decision can be made in an instant.

Right now. Or right now. Or right now.

Any moment is the right moment to adjust your alignment. And once you decide, you give permission once again to the fulfillment of your dream, your goal, and your purpose.

And how do my tiny choices have anything to do with the level of success I'm able to attain (and maintain) in my life?

I'm glad you asked.

Champions don't become champions in the ring, they are merely recognized there. Success is merely the evidence to the level of discipline and commitment you've held up. It's like physical muscles are proof of your commitment to work out every day.

Champions don't become champions in the ring, they are merely recognized there.

Star athletes became a champion every time they said yes to their dream, got up early, finished their workout routine, and did what others were not willing to do in order to better themselves. Your success or failure is hidden in your daily routine. That's where it all happens. If you cheat there, it will come out eventually.

Former heavyweight champion, Joe Frazier, said, "You can map out a fight plan, but when the action starts, it boils down to reflexes. That's where your road work shows. If you've cheated on that in the dark of the morning, you'll get found out under the bright lights."

You can map out a fight plan, but when the action starts, it boils down to reflexes. That's where your road work shows. ~Joe Fraizer

This is a perfect analogy for success in every area of our lives. It's all about what you do when no one is watching. It's about what you do to prepare. Do you walk in excellence? Do you operate in integrity? Are all your choices bringing you closer to the fulfillment of your dream? Okay, now let's go back to the chapter title, "If it's worth having, it's hard to get."

This statement is both true and untrue at the same time. The bottom line is any choice you make has 'hard' attached to it:

Choice#1: If you choose to live with intention and fulfill your destiny, it will be hard. Things will come against you. You'll often have to go against the status-quo. You may feel lonely at times and without encouragement. You'll need self-discipline, commitment, and to constantly remind yourself that you can do this. You'll have to give yourself pep-talks and learn how to quickly realign yourself when you start to drift off course. Are all these things hard? Absolutely!

Choice#2: If you choose to slack off, settle for less than you are capable of or become complacent, it will be hard. You'll constantly wonder what you could have achieved if you had only changed your habits and said yes to your dreams. You'll regret the fact that you never stepped out of your comfort zone long enough to experience the thrill of success. It will be hard to look at your life one day and wonder what you could have been, if only you would have given yourself permission.

If you look at it this way, I'm sure you'll agree that both choices are hard. It's just that one comes with the promise of a fulfilled life and the ability to walk in freedom while the other comes with disappointment and regret.

Both paths are hard. My advice to you? Choose your hard.

Everything worthwhile is uphill.

*The greatest oak was once just a little nut
who held its ground.*

~ Anonymous

Action Exercises

What is the difference between being stubborn and being committed?

When you give up on something, how do you explain it to yourself? Do you identify good reasons why you are stopping?

What is the upside of giving up in these areas?

What is the downside of giving up in these areas?

Write out the answers, or think about them, or better yet, discuss them with a loved one.

11

Where is my why?

The two most important days of your life are the day you were born, and the day you find out why.

~ Mark Twain

Each one of us was created with a purpose. There is an internal version of you that is fully equipped with unique gifts, talents, and passions. This true version of yourself can be suppressed, starved, and ignored or it can be nurtured and given the freedom to grow. The choice is yours.

You're not a carbon copy of anyone else. If you were, you'd be dispensable. Anyone could fill your shoes and your purpose in life. But they absolutely cannot.

We complicate things, don't we? I think the fact that we are thinking and reasoning adults is sometimes our downfall, especially when it comes to finding our 'why.' We start out as children filled with wonder and optimism. Children say things like, "I want to fly. I want to touch the stars. I want to live under water." The possibilities for children is limitless, they have no sense of 'the impossible.' Limitations are learned later in life. As parents, it's our job to nurture our children's dreams and encourage them to follow their natural bent. There are numerous childhood development studies that outline the benefits of allowing your child to search, explore, and follow their dreams.

The Bible provides some awe-inspiring insight into this way of thinking. Proverbs 18:16 assures us, "A man's gifts will make room for him."

Your gift is that divine spark that you were born with. It is that certain something you were created to live out and be. Your gift is connected to your purpose, your passion, and ultimately your ability to live a fulfilled life. It is all wrapped up in your big 'why.'

When you're operating in your gift and walking out your purpose it doesn't matter how difficult the journey is. It doesn't matter how much time it takes to evolve or become exactly what you are called to be. Money, education, and time invested in your purpose don't feel like a sacrifice to you because it's what you are meant to do! There is an inner passion connected to our purpose!

German philosopher Friedrich Nietzsche said, "He who has a why to live for can bear almost any how."

How long? How difficult? How much will it cost? How far will I have to go? How much more will I have to learn? How many more obstacles will I face? These things don't matter when you have your 'why!'

He who has a why to live for

can bear almost any how.

~Friedrich Nietzsche

It's interesting to take note of the fact that the Scripture doesn't say, "Your education will make room for you." Now, I fully believe in educating yourself, but if education alone was the secret to a fulfilled life then everyone with a degree would be living out the best version of themselves. Today's statistics on career fulfillment prove otherwise. Gallup surveys show that over 60% of the working population across all career tracks, educational levels, and industries are "not engaged" or are "actively disengaged" from their work. It's not that we as a whole have lost our ability to connect with meaningful work. I believe the answer to this disengagement is the fact that most of us are not living out our purpose. The work we are doing might be meaningful to the right person, but not to us!

When we actively suppress the part of our being that wants to dream and grow while instead forcing ourselves onto paths that we imagine to be less risky or more practical we are settling for a life we were never meant to live. You can have all the education in the world, but if you're not actively reaching toward your individual life purpose something will always feel 'off.' It is that unsatisfied and persistent worrying that many of us can't put our finger on.

The good news here is that your 'why' is right where you left it and you can pick it up at any moment. You have an internal compass that can still be accessed. It's the place where your dreams are still alive.

So the question then becomes, "Where is my why and how do I find it?"

Your journey to your 'why' truly begins when you make that first decision in awareness. The moment you say to yourself, "I will give myself permission to find and live out my life purpose," the entire universe conspires together to bring it to pass. You move from darkness to light by one choice. The follow-up actions you take will reveal themselves along the way. It begins with the decision to actively disengage from everyone else's expectations and allow yourself to fully access that inner child who was allowed to dream big.

Think about it. Do you remember the last time you woke up with a true sense of purpose? Or have you been operating as a slave to the deadlines and constant flood of distractions offered up by the influences around you? Remember, in an earlier chapter you learned that you have to be the protector of your own brain. It goes deeper than just focusing on positive thoughts and believing in yourself. You also have to agree to protect the vision and purpose that you've been given—even if it hasn't fully revealed itself yet.

It's as simple as this: The key to walking is to continue to walk. Once you decide to live out your purpose you will naturally find yourself in positions where you will have opportunities to choose to nurture your dreams. You will also have opportunities to suppress them. It is a continual choice you are making with every step. "But how will I know?"

This is where most people get stuck. Many of us aren't used to accessing our internal compass. It seems too New Age to nurture a path unknown. "What if I make a mistake? What if I fail?" See the vicious cycle? This kind of thinking will have you right back in the grip of fear. Fear of the unknown is what keeps us in the bondage of settling for far less than we were created to be.

The truth is, you don't have to know exactly how it will all come together. I can actually promise you that you won't! Your biggest responsibility in this process of becoming is to choose to say yes to your purpose every day without putting a cap on your dreams.

Everything else will come to you. Why? Because as you begin to say yes to your true purpose and give yourself permission to live free from the prison you've put yourself in, you will begin to see your goals and dreams with ever increasing clarity. The fact that you want to see them is all it takes for them to begin to appear. The more you say yes, the more will be revealed. You've only been stuck all this time because you made a decision to leave your dreams and goals behind. You lost your 'why' when you traded your purpose for something that seemed easier or more secure.

Compromise will always be offered up to you, so get used to that. However, as you continue to live a life intent on fulfilling your purpose the voices of the things you used to settle for will begin to sound more ridiculous.

It's like the guy who pushed against all odds to become the first entrepreneur in his family. He started out cutting his neighbor's lawn and now ten years later he has seven crews who are responsible for all the golf-course properties in his town. What would happen if someone walked up to him and offered him a secure management job with an hourly pay rate? If entrepreneurship is connected to his 'why' and he is living out his purpose, he would laugh at that offer. Sure, it may seem like less work, less responsibility, and a guaranteed paycheck but in reality this man's passion is already attached to his business. He is fulfilled. He is continuing to grow. In fact, he just provided two jobs last month to young men who are in the community re-entry program. These men served time in jail and now are receiving a second chance at life. This extra layer of fulfillment further connects this entrepreneur to his 'why.' Do you think he knew he'd be helping change lives when he first felt that inner pull to start his own lawn service company? Of course not, but he had the courage to follow his inner compass. He decided to say yes to that pull.

Where is your inner compass pointing you? If you choose to listen and continue to give yourself permission to live out your greatest purpose you will find it because it's already within you.

Good judgement comes from experience.
Experience comes from bad judgement.

~ Will Rogers

Action Exercises

Do you know why you are here?

Are you happy to not know why you are here?

Do you know anyone who passionately pursues their purpose?

What difference does it make in their life?

If you don't know your purpose, are you spending some time every day looking for it?

Write out the answers, or think about them, or better yet, discuss them with a loved one.

12

Summary

God doesn't require us to succeed;
He only requires that you try.
                    ~ Mother Teresa

If you've got this far through the book, I'm guessing you're ready for the next marvelous chapter of your life. It's time for a change, right? Another ten years on autopilot is just not an option any more.

I used to lay in bed thinking to myself, "I wonder what I'm capable of if I really threw myself into something with all my might?"

And it was a comforting thought for a while. It took me away from the humdrum of my daily disappointing existence; but inevitably I had to return at some point.

The interesting thing was that I somehow thought that the only requirement for my dream life to unfold was for me to be discovered; that someone would spot my genius and then everything would be alright! How can you delude yourself to that extent?

Eventually I came to the realization that nothing is going to happen unless I make it happen. No one is going to discover you. No one is going to make it easy for you. No one is going to take away the pain. You have to do it for yourself.

For some people that might be bad news. Yet, when you think about it this means your new life can begin any moment you choose. You are not waiting for anyone.

Your life may be dark and disappointing, but hope begins in the dark.

Hope is being able to see that there is light despite all of the darkness ~Desmound Tutu

You may be worried about failing. You may be concerned about being disappointed if things don't work out as you want it to. Well, you will be disappointed because you will fail. But failure is temporary if you keep going. And what's the alternative? You are certainly doomed if you don't even try.

You may be worried about what other people will say. And it's true, you may well be in for ridicule and criticism from those who lack your courage not to settle for a stagnant life.

Remember though, those who never made a mistake never tried anything new. There is only one way to avoid criticism: do nothing. This means do nothing, say nothing, and ultimately be nothing. It's obvious where that will lead.

You may criticize yourself for not having started all this years ago thinking it's too late now. Wrong. No matter how old you are, you have the rest of your life ahead of you. It is pure folly not to go after a goal because of the amount of time it will take to achieve it. Why? Because the time is going to pass anyway!

A great example of this was King David. He had a dream to build a Temple for God but it was not possible. Did he let his dream go away, no! He shared his dream with his son Solomon and the temple was built. His dream became a reality through his son.

Maybe you could have started years ago. Perhaps the very best time to begin would have been ten or even twenty years ago. But you didn't, so the second-best time is right now. It's never too late to become what you could have been!

Too many of us are not living our dreams
because we are too busy living our fears.
~ Les Brown

Why don't more of us go for it then? My friend Les Brown says that too many of us are not living our dreams because we are living our fears. (He also said that the tiger doesn't concern himself with the opinion of the sheep, which although it doesn't fit here, I love it!) We can't afford to allow fear to hold us back. We have to find a way to go after our dreams because if we don't then we will spend our time working for someone else, building their dreams for them.

We don't need to be a genius and we don't need to be an overnight success. It doesn't matter how long it takes us or how slowly we go, as long as we don't give up and don't stop.

We need to find the motivation to keep moving forward, to go from one failure to the next with no loss of enthusiasm.

The more we persist the more we develop character. And character is ours to keep.

You need to go out and say to the world: "No more limits!

If we are going to be successful in living out our dream life then we have to stand up straight and look life in the eye. We need to take part. We need to go out and live without limits!

Probably the happiest I've seen my child is after it has been raining. He goes outside on our driveway or in front of the house and then jumps in the water puddles. The sheer delight in his face is beyond the comprehension of the adult mind – at least it is mine. He would jump in those puddles for hours if we'd let him. Finally, when he is soaked and cold, we drag him back inside. Still, he cries because we have ruined his experience.

How do we become so paralyzed and unadventurous in adult life? Why are we so worried about messing up, making mistakes, or appearing foolish?

As my mentor John Maxwell says, "No one is good at anything the first time." If we are going to try new things, we are going to make mistakes.

And that's ok! That's good!

As we take part in life we learn and grow. But I'm talking about more than just doing something different. That is change, but change is not enough. Change is doing something different but transformation is *being* something different.

I'm talking about being something different tomorrow than you are today.

More than that, evolution is a continual transformation, a continual growth, and a continual change. This is what we need.

I believe that's why we're here: to experience life and to learn and grow from our experiences. I believe we are here to grow physically, mentally, and spiritually.

I adopted my 'mission' in life from a mentor of mine several years ago—to be all that I can be for myself, my fellow man, and for God.

And I firmly believe that the only way any of us can do that is by living life to the fullest—by going out and living life with no more limits.

I believe that is our responsibility to live. We don't need to worry about doing it perfectly.

We are responsible for the effort, not the result.

We can't control a great deal about the world and all the other people in it, but we can control our own efforts. We can all do our best and that's all it takes.

Good luck and may God bless you on your journey. Start now and go as far as you can see. When you get there you'll see how to go further.

Thank you for buying this book and reading it! If you would like to find out more about some of our other learning resources, go to:

carlosvargas.com

vipleadershipgroup.com

You can follow us in social media:

https://www.linkedin.com/in/cavarpe

https://twitter.com/cavarpe

https://fb.com/carlosvargasvip